Ancestral

Daniel Smith

Ancestral

Daniel Smith

Water's Edge Press

Copyright © 2021 by Daniel Smith

All rights reserved.

Printed in the United States of America

Water's Edge Press LLC
Sheboygan, WI
watersedgepress.com

ISBN: 978-1-952526-03-9

Library of Congress Control Number: 2021931319

Credits
From *The Orchard* by Theresa Weir, copyright © 2011. Reprinted by permission of Grand Central Publishing, an imprint of Hachette Book Group, Inc.

Quotation from Michael Mott from a letter to the author, May 14, 2017.

Cover photo by the author; artistic design by Ryan M. Smith, MD. Photo of Smith home from family archives.

Other images licensed through VectorStock.

A WATER'S EDGE PRESS FIRST EDITION

For Cheryl

Acknowledgements

Acorn Whistle: "Poem for Cheryl"

The Kerf: "Note to the Hired Hand"

Midwestern Gothic: "Father's Day" and "Northwestern Illinois in June"

The Midwest Quarterly: "Anvil"

Tundra and *Narrative Magazine*: "What Gary Snyder Said to Me, That Day, in the Doorway of the Milking Barn"

The Prairie Wind: "Wet Spring"

Seems: "Some Nights, My Father," "Texas, 1974," and "The Fields in Winter"

The following poems appeared in a chapbook, *Fatherland*, published by Longhouse Publishers & Booksellers: "Plowman," "Vesper," "Note to the Hired Hand," "Texas, 1974," "Father's Day," and "Summer, 2006."

Special thanks to Bottom Dog Press for publication of my book of poems, *Home Land*, as part of the Human Landscapes Trilogy of Poems, as well as inclusion in the *Bottom Dog Press Poetry Anthology 25th Anniversary*.

Special thanks also to the National Endowment for the Arts and the American Composers Forum for supporting Patrick Beckman's musical composition of my poems as part of the *Continental Harmony: New Music for the Millennium* national creative project in the year 2000.

Author's Note

These poems grew from the life Robert and Mary Smith provided my siblings and me on the farm near Freeport, Illinois that was home for so many years. It was a precious and enduring gift that I was later fortunate to share with my wife, Cheryl, and our sons, Austin, Ryan, and Levi. May these poems help my parents' legacy live on to enrich the lives of my grandchildren, future generations of the Smith family, and all who care deeply about lives lived close to the land.

Leaving the family farm brought inevitable heartache but also provided the opportunity to set down roots in the beautiful Driftless Region of Southwestern Wisconsin and to work as a counselor to farm families in crisis across the state. Their voices can be heard in these poems, and I am fortunate to have had the opportunity to assist them.

I am extremely grateful to those who have encouraged, advised, and supported my writing over the years, especially Austin Smith, a master poet in his own right, along with J.D. Whitney, Gary Snyder, Roger Dunsmore, Wendell Berry, Ed Janus, Larry Backe, Michael Theune, and Allen Redford. I treasure the memory of the late poets Michael Mott and Lucien Stryk, who taught me the way, and in doing so, provided friendship and guidance. I miss you both dearly.

Thank you to Water's Edge Press, and specifically my editor, Dawn Hogue, for bringing *Ancestral* to print.

And finally, to Cheryl and our family—Austin, Ryan and Trang, Levi and Brenna, and our dear grandchildren—my love and deepest appreciation for being part of the journey.

Table of Contents

One

Remembrance 1
Anvil 2
The Day 3
Plowman 4
A Farmer Dies in Springtime 5
The Woods 6
Two 7
Then and Now 8
Hiking Through the Pandemic 9
What Gary Snyder Said to Me, That Day,
in the Doorway of the Milking Barn 10
Father's Day 11
To Age 12
The Waves 13
Our Fields Are So Wet: Notes from
a Northern Wisconsin Farmwife 14

Two

The Red Fox 25
Summer, 2006 26
A Faith 27
Vesper 28
Chores at Dawn 29
Craftsmanship 30
Note to the Hired Hand 32
Northwestern Illinois in June 33
Farm Work 34
Poem for Cheryl 35
Texas, 1974 36
Walking 38
Wet Spring 39
Farm Classified 40
On My 66th Birthday 41
For a Friend, Lost 42
This Morning 43
A Gathering of Waters 44

Three

On a Sunday in January...... 53
Hummingbird...... 54
Spring Night...... 55
A Gift...... 56
Driving Home...... 58
Between Generations...... 60
Corncrib Carpenter...... 61
August 2, 2020...... 62
Evening on Knight Hollow...... 63
To Pause...... 64
After Your Reading...... 65
November 22, 1963...... 66
Landmarks...... 67
Searching...... 68
At Dusk, in My Father's Barn...... 69
In the Fall of My Life: Words of a Bachelor Farmer...... 70
No Human Sound...... 73

Four

Ancestral...... 77
Estranged...... 78
January 31, 2010...... 79
Dry Dirt...... 80
Holy Water...... 81
Changing Weather...... 82
Coming In...... 83
Next Year...... 84
For Levi...... 85
To My Deceased Parents...... 86
Chasing Chores...... 87
Crisis Call...... 88
Cultivating...... 89
old farmer...... 90
Some Nights, My Father...... 91
The Fields in Winter...... 92
Our Winter House...... 99

The Smith family home on the farm near Freeport, IL, circa 1941.

"There was immeasurable comfort in knowing this would be the rest of your life. And there was immeasurable sorrow in knowing this would be the rest of your life. In knowing that, when you were gone, the plow would still cut deep into the ground you once planted. Fields that had been everything to you would still exist after you were gone. Maybe not in the same way. Maybe not with the same poetry, but they would exist."

Theresa Weir, *The Orchard*

"Every loss is a liberation and every liberation is a loss."

Michael Mott, author of *Counting The Grasses* and *The Seven Mountains of Thomas Merton*

One

Remembrance

Now and again
all that was
comes back to me
across the miles and days
laid end to end
as if to show the way
and sometimes I go
though I know
what was
cannot be again
and perhaps
in part
never was
though right now
alone
in a distant field
it appears so close
my arms spread wide
cannot begin
to hold it all.

Anvil

I've hauled my father's anvil
due north
up out of the black Illinois farm ground
he and I together worked,
decades our home.

Set down sixty pounds
onto the floor of this old barn,
new only to me.

All around, our bewildered tools
hang in the strange light
of the cracked windowpane

where I stand
looking out over land
not yet home.

It is growing late
on a late winter's day.

At my feet, my father's anvil,
his striking song of steel on steel
still hammering home.

The Day

How abruptly change appears
Dressed as wildfire leaping the divide,
Or the armed intruder in the hall,
Or the drunk driver failing to stop.

So the norm is now respite.
The blessed day the day that ends
As it began—everything you love
Intact, at peace, safely home.

Plowman

He filled one room
of a fallen down farmhouse
with a cot, table, and chair.

Cooked on hot plate
his dinner of bacon and beans.

All winter scratched the frost
from the windowpane,
watching for spring.

When finally,
the fields were fit,
he limped out on bad hips
to start up the tractor and plow.

His eyes set
on the far end of a twenty-acre field,
the first furrows trailing behind
like smoke.

A Farmer Dies in Springtime

Home from the hospital
To a bed
With a view of the fields.

Tended by hospice,
Who arrive morning and night,
Like a hired man come to chore.

Neighbors stop by, sit bedside,
Stare into their hands,
Red and cracked from winter.

They recall the year
Of the early frost, flood
Or big drought.

They avoid talk
Of the plowing or planting,
Of the futures for cattle or corn.

The tractor, disc, and planter
Stay locked in the shed
With seed bought months ago

When the new catalogs arrived,
Glossy with promise and primed
For a year that would not be.

The Woods

Sunday morning, the path
winds beneath bare branches
of aspen, oak, elm, and linden.

My sons follow, trusting
I'll bend back brambles,
cast blocking limbs aside.

Wide-eyed, silent,
they see these five acres
of woods on Grandpa's farm
        as wilderness.

I want to tell them
value nothing more
than you value these woods.

Its floor of acorns
        and leaves.
Its sky of arched trees.

But instead, only promise
to walk often
in sacred procession,

visitors, explorers, seekers
in this holy land
of rabbit, squirrel, deer, and fox.

Two

Each day, on my way
Between home and work
I pass the very spot
Where we first met.

Nearly a half century
Yet the black iron railing
Where you knelt beside your bike
Remains bolted in place.

All these years and all has changed
But how we met and how we felt
As we spoke our first words
And set out together toward today.

Now come nights when I wake
And reach across the darkness
Touching you I settle safely
Back to who and what we have become.

It is then I thank the stars, the sun and moon,
The wind and rain, the growing grass and every
Little thing everywhere that merged and forged
Two diverse worlds onto one never-ending path.

Then and Now

I dreamt of living
Alone
On the farthest ridge.

Raking a garden
Smooth
In the stony soil.

Reeling
In the high, clear air.

While far below
The world spun round
And round
On muddy wheels,
Running its race.

Then, one day, in a doorway,
You turned
And I
Turned back
And knew at once
I was home.

Hiking Through the Pandemic

Heading west
Above Stewart Lake
Early Sunday morning

I came upon
A lone hiker heading east
Backpack, hiking poles

He stepped back into the brush
So that we might pass
Six feet apart

We wished each other good health
Went on through the spring flowers
Birdsong, bull frogs calling from the lake

One brief passing
On a trail in the woods, enough
To rejoin what has gone asunder

What Gary Snyder Said to Me, That Day, in the Doorway of the Milking Barn

I am going to tell you
what you need to do.

You need to teach these cows
to meditate.

To lose their bodies
in a trance for, say,
five days.

Then they will need no feed.
They will give no milk.

And you can leave
and come out to see me,

and I can show you
my trees.

Father's Day

I watched my father when I
was a boy. I watched my father and followed
my father all morning through chores,
the long morning chores leading into the day,
the day's farm work and fieldwork.

I watched my father and followed my father
and at high noon I followed him in to wait behind
him at the wash tub in the old farmhouse.

He used tough bars of Lava soap
and a horse bristle brush clean up to his elbows.
His sunburnt arms red and hay chaff specked,
the hot scrubbing before the cold water rinse
of the morning's work,
be it cattle or crop, metal or wood.

I watched and followed
my father all those years and now
decades have passed since I touched his hand.

I live on land my father never saw, miles
and miles from all we knew. Each morning I rise
to the barn and fields—these chores I do
to keep me sane.

Come noon, I am
the man at the wash tub, lathering
and rising, lathering and rinsing.

To Age

So many lessons learned
As a child
I no longer believe

The old voices fade
Like the singing
Of a distant choir

Now I have begun
To set aside things
Too heavy to carry

As the trail climbs
Up from the dense woods
Onto open ground

And I find myself
Six decades out
Trying on new lives

Like one does a new coat
When the days darken
And winter draws close

The Waves

What was home
all those years
in all weathers the work
coming in waves
until whole lives
and loves
washed out
onto open water
the familiar land
receding
growing small
like an island
left behind
while adrift
unsure of direction or fate
I felt the tightening
grip of time
until washing up
onto good soil
and somehow finding
legs enough
to rise up
and walk.

Our Fields Are So Wet: Notes from a Northern Wisconsin Farmwife

I.

I will never live a normal life.

Still, this is what I'd like to try—
find someone to buy part of the farm
let us live here
and do what we've always done.

What else can we do?

My youngest is coming back from Afghanistan.
After discharge she'll have all summer.
She could help out some, I would think.

There's not much else. My oldest says
just wait until everyone is home, then
figure out what to do.

But then, just when I get Wayne to where
he is somewhat normal, Mom starts in
and we all come around to the same mess again.

I was talking to the neighbor who says
Mom thinks I'm listening in on her phone calls
but I'm not. I've got enough problems of my own.

The grandson was here last week. I loved it.
He might be back sometime, maybe.

Other than that, I'm just waiting
for the ground around the house to dry

and some warm weather
so that I can work some dirt.
I'd like to garden for the daughter—
with two kids Lord knows she'll need the food.

But still, not sure what or how to do
what everyone wants. I think
I'll talk to some of the farmers around here, see
if maybe, they can help with fieldwork.

Son Ben found a job, but it is in Texas.
Not sure when he's leaving but it could be soon.

If it would just dry up
we could turn the heifers out before he goes,
cut down on some of the chores.

Wayne is getting shots in his back on Tuesday.

When we were talking, that day at the house,
you mentioned the big outfits that buy land
and let the family live on there—please tell them
I'm ready to talk.

II.

Not sure of much.

Son Ben is gone.
Yep, left this morning after chores.

So, it has come to this:
Kids grown. Body shot. Social life shattered.

Wayne says he has to do some thinking.

I asked him questions but he is unsure of what to do.
I told him about getting hired help or something like that.
He said he has to think
but there is little time for thinking
and our fields are so wet.
I called a realtor in Spooner.
He is going to make some calls,
will let me know in a few days.
Still unsure of what to do
but I am looking.

Wayne's brother is going to talk to him today.
He's driving Wayne home
from getting shots in his back
and will talk about stuff—
see if he can get in Wayne's brain.

III.

Well, how life does change in a short time.

Our son has been gone since Easter.
Last night on the phone I asked him point blank,
Are you coming home for winter?
His answer—no—only to snowmobile
then straight back south.

So here I am again.

Wayne lost it
when I told him the neighbor come by
asking what we are going to do.
I told him depends on our son
but now I know the answer to that.
The banker says he will leave the note open
just like a line of credit
so we have options.

Now I have to go tell the neighbor
our son is not coming home
and I need to start thinking
about what was talked about.

Wayne is in bad shape today,
his back again. I told him we need to do something.
Can't keep on going like we are
but he was in no shape to listen.

I went to mow lawn and he came out back
stopped me to ask if we are going to plant corn.
I said I guess—so he is plowing now.
We have one field done and two small ones to go.

If the rain would just hold off a bit
it would be nice.

Wayne was not happy yesterday
but today, after riding the tractor
and doing the plowing
he seems better.

This is what it looks like:
We owe the bank 70 thousand
FHA another 26 and still 30 thousand to Dad.

The banker says we should talk
and I want to but there is so much work
it's all I can do every day.
We got the heifers turned out
but still have 30 cows in the milking barn.
The silo is running empty and
no hay. I went ahead, rented out half the farm
and got a down payment on the other half.
We close in November.

I'm okay but still get the panic attacks
now and then.

Wayne is not worth talking about
but he knows what we need to do.
He just can't comprehend at times.
When the kids see him
they get so upset at how he acts.

I hope things change.
I wish I could just get away.

I am looking at part time work
like maybe a school aid
or clerk at the country market in Spooner.
I talked to the manager but all he has is night shift.

IV.

Well, I'm fine.

Won't talk about my other half.

His brain trauma is taking a toll.
He tries to tell me things people said
that they never did.

The cows will be sold on the 22nd.
The kids are helping me as
Wayne is a daily struggle and now,
his good friend from hunting and snowmobiling
died travelling out west.
Just laid down to nap and never woke up.
Would have turned 52 in August.

It is hard but I'm surviving.

Wayne better wake up.
I'm tired of his act.
Maybe another med change might help.

V.

Just letting you know the cows are gone.
Yep, just finished loading them.
Told the dealer to send the check after the first of the year.

Never saw Wayne move so fast as when the trucks pulled in.
He sure never moved that fast before.

So now just cleaning up junk
and hauling to recycle.

I want a new house. Move Mom in here
so she isn't alone all the time.
The county says the house is not worth fixing
so I'm figuring in a book
how to afford a new one.

VI.

Boy you wouldn't believe
how bad it gets.
Wayne can't be reasoned with and now
we have four funerals to get to—one tomorrow
in Tomahawk then another in Green Bay.
Two more in Spooner after that.

Wayne says he'll come, too, but I wish
he'd just stay put. I need time away to think.

I wish his new meds would kick in.
The pharmacy forgot to renew his morphine

and no one noticed so he was in withdrawal yesterday.
Wow, was that bad.
But I'm still here and he is getting oxy now.

Keep me in your prayers.

VII.

Ready to pull my hair out.
Does that seem normal?

The old house got torn down today
so we are living in a shed out back.

Wayne is helping a neighbor chop corn.

I hope I got everything back to the state,
all that paperwork and permits.
Then we can start on a basement and wood burner.

Winter is coming. You can feel the cold.

VIII.

Oh, I have to tell you
this is so nice compared to what we had.

Wayne still trouble. Only goes out
to doctor appointments and when he does
I go for a walk. I just stand in the sun and look back
at our new basement house.

I wish the weather would hold. I wish it would stay
this way all winter.

But I know Wayne is far from well.

I never hear from son Ben way down in Texas.
Hardly ever see the girls who live nearby.

I know the big lake storms are coming.

I know I will never have a normal life.

Two

The Red Fox

for my grandchildren

I saw a red fox
drinking from the horse pail
in the pasture
south of the barn.

A winter sunset blazed
upon his hide
and his black ears
pointed toward the early stars.

Suddenly aware, he bolted
for the dark woods
but I did not follow.
It was enough

to know he exists,
to know this world
still shelters
the rare and the wild.

Summer, 2006

for Austin, in Alaska

We'll share these stars,
the cycles of the moon,
the sound of rain
starting up on the trees.

The north wind
you'll feel first.

While I, alone in some pasture,
calling cows
long before sunup,
will scan the skies
for the Northern Lights.

Aurora Borealis.

And come to realize
should you stir
in your tent
to peer out at the night sky,

you and I
could be admiring them
together.

A Faith

You awaken, and worry
comes to your face
with the light
through the window.

I am sorry
I am never there.

You ask, when we meet,
what will we do tomorrow?
Where will we live?

I have no good answers.
I can only point
to the new grass
rising
in the hill pastures,

and promise, if the rains come
again, and again,
the year will carry us
with it.

Vesper

That we be out in the open
afoot in the fields
as the breeze bends the brome,
as the earth cools, belonging more
to night than day.

That we stand
with leaf and branch
deep in the heart of woods
as darkness descends
to hold us
as we hold each other
in one embrace of evening.

That as our eyes fill
our ears fill
with the songs of bobwhite
and ringtail
floating from fencerows,
catching in a net of song
an audience of two.

That we walk home
to a house in the hills
of land that we love, and love
in a bed of marriage,
trusting the dark sky's return
to light,
when we'll rise, rested,
in love with the new day.

Chores at Dawn

The milking barn waits
below the hill.

I walk the wet pasture
one hour before dawn,
herding Holsteins.

A few stars overhead.
Corn leaves bend in the breeze.
My steps move the cows
into a single file line.

I think of worlds
I've not lived in and languages
I cannot speak.

Shaped now by routine,
I've hung it all
from stars above a quiet pasture.

My life's work
sketched by cow trails
into this ground
I call my home.

Craftsmanship

for my sons

These are just chores.
I've told you that, time and again.

It is what we do
when we rise in the morning
and head out, ready
and able
to take on whatever
the day
puts before us.

Equipped with all you have
studied,
crafted,
absorbed, and perfected,
through the dedicated hours
that led you
down the long path of practice.

So that now
you hold in your hands,
hearts, and minds,
the defined tools of your
craftsmanship.

Able to diagnose
the emerging illness,
elusive solution, or perfected phrase.

Afoot on your daily rounds,
mind and body
determined to assist
the student, client,
or patient.

No difference
from all those chores
we tackled, side-by-side,
together,

as we tended the sickly calf,
or the withering crop,
or the rusted chain
we feared might break.

Note to the Hired Hand

The gate you left open
the pony found.

I spotted her at dawn
knee deep in alfalfa.

Drunk on feed and freedom
she fled
I chased
one half hour through morning rain.

You'll find her now
back in the barn,
waiting to be brushed.

Northwestern Illinois in June

We want the rain
not the wind
my father would say
as we watched the big storms
born of Iowa afternoon heat
come across
the Mississippi
only to turn north
into Wisconsin
showing us
their flash of heat lightning
like the lighted windows
of passing trains
behind
the night sky clearing
opening to stars
as we turned to go in
our footsteps
breaking the brittle grass
the oak leaves
turned white and upward
like a beggar
holding an empty bowl.

Farm Work

Day follows day
over this land like water
downstream over rock, sand, sediment.

All a man can do
is put one foot before the other,
pull his hat down tight.

Each spring, the frost-heaved stones
rise from the plowing,
point to all that needs doing.

Then, from season to season, I live
as wire
pulled taut from post to post.

Beneath, in the tall grass,
whole worlds slip by, felt
but never seen.

Poem for Cheryl

We awoke
to sleet slashing the trees,
the tent
flapping in horizontal wind.

Gathered clothes, sleeping bags—
walked back, arm-in-arm,
two miles
to the old farmhouse.

All day shivering, dreaming
in the gray light
of the rented windows.

All we have today
        was sown then—

And rises now like flowers
piercing new ground
        April's first warm day.

Texas, 1974

Halfway through
the first good week of harvest—
North Texas dry land wheat—
the combine snapped a shaft.

With a kick and a cuss, the boss
left for parts,
80 miles round trip.

Old Texan Harry Martin—
wheat rancher, cattleman, oil driller—
offered a hand, so he and I
started in
tearing the big Gleaner down—
backing off belts,
loosening chains,
pulling bearings.

The tools hot in our hands,
on our backs
in the cheat grass,
shirts soaked, fire ants
at our ankles,
grasshoppers leaping in the heat.

Till an hour later, we took a break,
and there, in the shade
of the heavy traction wheels
he wanted to know
"What's a college boy like you
doing cutting wheat?"
I told him I'd never been this far west,
wanted to see the country.

Harry Martin.
His body brown and bent
as old mesquite,
stared with eyes calm as summer fallow
over miles of endless wheat,
spit between his boots and said,
"You know kid, I really don't think you would have missed
a goddamn thing."

Walking

Along these trails
Through foreign fields
Over uncertain landscapes

I follow my father's advice
To just keep putting
One foot before the other

Though I cannot name
The trees and grasses
Passed along the way

And the loons
Call from Bakken's Pond
In a language I will never learn

While the past drags behind
Like a heavy chain
I have no way to break

And all that is certain
Is one footfall at a time
On a pathway narrow and strange

Wet Spring

Two weeks now
we haven't turned a wheel.

The moldboard and disc
rust in the rain.
Tractors idle
in the cold sheds as
all day, the fields
gather
beneath seamless clouds.

One year ago
the corn stood ankle-high.

Sitting on a sack of seed, my father
—five decades of farming—swears
if we still farmed with horses
we'd have this crop in the ground.

The rest of the day, tinkering
with cold engines while the rain
worked the tin roof,
I hold this picture in my mind—

my father, at my age,
the sun in his hair,
check planting corn
behind a dapple mare.

Farm Classified

Desperate 56-year-old
Wisconsin farmer put farming first,
now wants wife. Seeks Protestant lady
with Wesleyan heritage 30 to 45.
Likes history, philosophy, unadorned lifestyle.
New house in '95.

On My 66th Birthday

I awaken and shun the news
I already know

There is illness poverty abuse
Nearby and around the globe

But along the Wolf Run Trail
Between Mazomanie and Black Earth

I hear only the murmurings
Of Black Earth Creek

I smell the corn in silk
And alfalfa someone just mowed

I come upon a mare with her spring foal
Grazing the glistening grass

These are small things
But today they are enough

To keep me walking celebrating
This day and all the days to come

For a Friend, Lost

for Dale, 1954 – 1979

Years later, I understand
why I hold to a trail
sliding downhill
through trees
to a streambank
turning white
with new snow
where you and I
stood
watching water
roll over rocks
unaware
of the hours passing
forever.

This Morning

I meant to wake you
To watch
With me
The full moon's
Reflection on the barn's
Tin roof.

But fell silent
Before
Your body—
A closed flower
Laid upon
A white sheet.

A Gathering of Waters

Evenings, all growing season,
all those years
when the table was cleared,
chairs pushed back,
we knelt on the hard pine floorboards
before the high crucifix
to pray for more rain,
to pray for less rain,
to pray the land stay
beneath our feet
the river within its banks.

As a child, up in my room,
sleepless through the hot nights,
I heard the grownups talking,
cooling down
over iced tea and beer, sitting out
on the dark porch
as the day's work slipped away.

Their stories going back—years back—
churning with old names,
faces barely remembered.

And everyone, everything
tied to the river that flowed
black and wild, right there,
a stone's throw from our door.

I overheard flood talk,
talk of water coming fast,
jumping the levee, covering the corn
and beans
and climbing the front steps
to the little world of rooms

I called home.

Floods like those, they told me
come once a century.
Floods like those
are not for you to worry.

The Mississippi. The Missouri.
Add all the little streams
feeding in—we trust God to keep them in place.
God—and the levees
we pushed up from the bottom fields.
Look! We build these houses
and we farm these fields
a stone's throw from the river's edge.

Then in '93 the spring came up
cold and wet
and summer followed just the same.
Two weeks rain—heavy up north—
and the old men
looked long and hard at the water, swore
Mother Nature had come to call.

Showers and thunderstorms—day after day—
all the Midwest staggering under the load
until all we owned, all we valued,
was gambled, homes chanced, crops planted,
lives built on land
borrowed from the river.

That was the year the river came calling,
filled with one downpour holding to another,
took back
what we once thought was ours.

───────────

In the midst of a summer day,
deep in work beside my father,
hoeing beans in the garden on land
that was our world,
we heard my mother call from the porch
the very words we most feared:

Heavy rain up river!

I saw my father rise from his tilling,
saw his shoulders fall
as if from some terrible weight.
It was, I knew, the weight of water.

———————

I speak the language of water,
of flowing water, past my family's home
there on Kaskaskia Island.

I've lived all my years
part of water, part of land
in a house perched on stilts
there on Kaskaskia Island.

Kaskaskia. Kaskaskia. Little island
that was my home.

Left out on its own
where water parted land
from land. Left out
where no one came calling—
the world just left us alone.

Until that summer of repeating rains, a summer
the sun couldn't seem to find—
land lost to water
and nothing to go back to.

Kaskaskia. Kaskaskia. Little island
that was my home.

———————

The last night the trains ran
the long light of the Burlington Northern
searched the wet rails, heading north
along the banks of the Great River, moving south.

From the levee
at the edge of the trembling town
I rose from my sandbagging,
from my futile labor
and heard the warning cry of the train's whistle:

Move back! Move Back! Give this river its reign!

———————

Mid-afternoon—a long line of thunderstorms
came down river.

Lightning chased us off the levee, left us
waiting out the rain, sipping cold coffee
in our trucks.

We watched the levee bend
and break right where we'd been working.

Silently, the trucks pulled out—taillights flickering
through the falling rain,
heading up onto the bluff road, moving up
onto higher ground.

———————

The river they say, will go wherever it wants.

A half-century of farming the flood plain
I know it is so.

Some years the best crops a man can grow.
Other years, the river takes it all.

After '86, I came back, picked up,
rebuilt the levees, took back my fields.

I am too old to go back now, to start over now.
If you were me, what would you do?

———————

Two weeks and two days
shoring up the levee at Jurgen Creek.

Toting sandbags, spreading straw.
One night nearly had a breach but swarmed through mud,
through rain, through the fear of losing it all—
and somehow, through night-long rain, it held.

All our lives thrown together, neighbor
helping neighbor, a chain of bodies
building a sandbag wall
against the flood of the century.

Home one night to clean up, to rest up
I heard the rain striking
tough as sleet
the tin roof overhead.

At midnight, a call from Jurgen Creek:

The levee broke! Get out! Get out!

We drove across the flat bottom fields
as the water flooded in,
already knowing we would never be back.

———————

Moved up out of the floodplain
to a house perched atop a limestone bluff.

A view downriver, out over the alder swamps
and the tops of cottonwoods.

Down there, I tell my little ones, down there
is where I lived.
It seems like a hundred lifetimes ago.

I tell them—no matter where you live,
make it home.

But I carry the weight of things lost,
of things swept away.

Now I've learned
to never get that close again.
I'll never fall in love with a place again.

No way could I stand to lose it all again.

———————

River of lifetimes spent in a river of work.
River of daydreams lost to a river of days.

River of my family, river of yours.
River that called us, carried us home.

River gone shallow in summers gone dry.
River freed from its basin by snowmelt and rain.

River born of oxbow lakes, gathering rivers along the way.
River of a thousand bends, bending back the way it came.

River of a nation, river of tribes.
River bringing comfort, river bringing tears.

———————

Moonlight over water. Moonlight over land.

I go out walking late in the night
on the levee that separates and protects.

It was the river geese that called me out.

I heard them passing overhead,
leaving the northland, heading south,
following the river south,
leaving the northland behind.

So much water flowing
down from the uplands,
heading south.

Years past high water.
Some lives restored with homes,
entire towns reset on solid ground.

This night, walking levees
out on my own
where land holds to water
and water to land,
I find the stain of past floods
pressed into the bluffs and tall trees—
a remembrance set hard and fast
above the black, sleeping water.

Three

On a Sunday in January

At twenty below
I keep the car running
While you shop for a few things:

Salad greens, French bread, and a Malbec
To go with the stew
We left simmering at home.

You come out
Holding the bags tight in your arms
The way one holds precious things.

You are smiling at some thought
While the wind sweeps your hair
Across the red of your lips

Turning my thoughts to spring
The garden south of the barn
Red cherry tomatoes ripening in sunlight.

Hummingbird

All summer, out
On the front deck,
I've lived in isolation.

Only you visited,
Darting beak first to the feeder,
Gorging on sugared water.

Now the walnuts and sumac
Have begun to fade.
The stars have turned autumnal.

In this world,
There are those who travel
And those who shelter in place.

We now know who we are.
You have the wings to carry you,
Southward, all the necessary miles.

While I turn inward, bracing
For the big storms of winter
And the long Wisconsin night.

Spring Night

Just today
I finished planting corn.

The last fields
worked in choking dust.
Seed set four inches deep
in a thin vein of dampness.

Today I meant to mow
first crop alfalfa,
but awoke at one a.m.
to rain at the window,
thunder rolling in.

My first real rest in weeks.

Eyes closed, I saw
thousands of corn seeds
trapped in dry dirt,
the rain reaching down
to pull them up.

A Gift

for Michael Mott

This friendship
born of a chance encounter
more than twenty years back.

I recall the day
brought the year's first snow.
We rushed out for a walk.

You told me of your book
Counting the Grasses
as I showed you my farm.

Our paths diverged
but we kept close
through letters and poems

which marked the years
like rings on a white oak
acknowledge aging and time.

Your letters now typed
as your perfect penmanship
fell to a trembling hand.

Still the occasional poem,
referenced work of art
or culture you wished to share.

And today, the perfect feather
of a black and white wren
held and admired,

and placed perfectly between pages
like one prepares
a rare and precious gift.

Driving Home

I passed a small herd of Black Angus
  standing broad shoulder to broad shoulder,
  heads bent to their evening feed,
    the first flakes of a big snow
        beginning to fall.

It took me back
  to my father in the fifties
    on the farm in northwestern Illinois.

He bought western feeder calves
  wide-eyed and green, right off the range,
    fed them out
    on silage and grain
    in a dirt lot back of the barn.

When fattened, shipped them off
    to the big stockyards in Chicago—
    steaks for businessmen
      on Michigan Avenue.

He rode the train in
    to watch them sell and bring back the check—
    money for new shoes, coats, schooling for eight kids.

My father gone now 20 years.

No one farms that way anymore.

They tore the stockyards out.

Still, those cattle
in a Wisconsin field
    bring it all back.

One of those things
we carry
and find impossible to leave
behind,

no matter where we are,
how we live,
who we've become.

Between Generations

We watch a red Illinois sunset
fall off beyond the house tops.

He sits with his gray head hung low,
talking acres of corn and peas,
a canning factory twenty years gone.

He knows every hillside farm
now subdivided
where corn tassels once waved.

He recalls the names of men who slept
on cots in cobbled corn cribs
those hot harvest nights.

Turning his hand, he shows me
how the pea pods hung on the vine,
how the corn struck the bang board wagons.

I smile and memorize this history
which flows to me through him.

The years have come and closed the fields
but in the late evening of his words
we are sunburned farmhands
driving a four-horse team.

Corncrib Carpenter

He has stepped back
out of August heat
into the noontime shade
of a cottonwood.

Perched on an upturned pail,
centered
in a square of broken boards,
he yanks spikes
and drips a steady stream.

His left ear cradles a pencil
thick as the cigar
joined to his lip.

A sixteen-ounce hammer
hangs from a hip.

He hoists a solid two-by
onto the stack marked SAVE.

He aims to build it
horse high, bull strong, hog tight—

whatever it is, he's building.

August 2, 2020

We walk this trail
Along and above the lake
Beneath poplar, spruce, and birch.

Forty years.
Children, and now, grandchildren.
Changing jobs, homes.

Walking, our one constant,
On and on, days and miles,
One foot before the other.

We've come this far together,
We'll go on, up hills, down valleys
As far as the trail will take us.

Evening on Knight Hollow

At dusk
Deer slip from the woods
Quiet as yarn through a needle.

They press pointed hooves
Into the soft soil
Beneath the soybeans.

Far down valley
A cow calls her calf
To come back.

Soon stars will appear
And stare down
On us all.

This is how it is,
How it has always been
On farms where I have lived.

If I smoked
I would light a cigarette
On a dark, open porch

Let it cut the darkness
So all would know
I am here and watching.

To Pause

for Lucien Stryk

At last
I have learned to pause
east of the barn
near the old stone wall
of a silo long fallen
beneath the swallows
taking flight
through the open doorway
the garden cooling
the June evening
turning inward
my breath
calm as the fading light
my thoughts
not going to any other place
or time
no forgotten or
unspoken language
no discarded task
or lingering remorse
only this night
filling with stars
that just now
I have found the wisdom
to accept

After Your Reading

for Forrest Gander

All day, the day
you travelled
      a thousand miles home,
I worked in the fields
      we had walked
           together, searching the stars.

For fence—bull strong, hog tight—
I set brace posts
      three feet deep
      onto bedrock.

Stretched barbed wire, barehanded
      with block and tackle
      taut and true, worthy
           to stand the years.

Alone, surrounded
by the solidity of field and fence,
I carried your language
over spring's new grass,
      careful and proud
      as a craftsman
carries his tools.

November 22, 1963

What is this
so cruel and dark

to have my mother
fingering her beads,

my father, at mid-day,
standing in the kitchen

silently staring
into an empty cup?

Landmarks

I have moved
a whole huge part of my life
into the past.

Loaded up a half century
of gatherings,
set out north
to this little patch of stony soil.

All around
the hills loom strange
to a flatlander.

Just now, the rain begins,
the wind bends low the pines.

And I, at the window
begin again, searching the vast valley

for my long-lost landmarks.

Searching

Each day
demands to be reckoned with.

These crossroads, walkways
of a new city,

of a new life, strange
as stepping out onto a new planet.

My cautious footfall
striking the unfamiliar pavement,

searching hallways, alleyways,
whole unmapped neighborhoods,

to gather what was scattered,
to own again what was lost.

Like once, as a child,
I searched the deep woods

for a wayward, newborn calf,
feeling all the while

the darkness descending,
the time running short.

At Dusk, in My Father's Barn

The long workdays
lay down
in the shadow
of the century-old beams.

The steel stanchions
swell with silence and the milk pails
hang empty
by the milk house door.

Up the ladder
in the great loft
where haymakers built
mountains of bales,
mice run
in the forgotten chaff
of the wide-planked floor.

While through the splintered walls
the lights
of the approaching town
                    intrude.

In the Fall of My Life: Words of a Bachelor Farmer

My grandparents gifted me this farm.
I call it a gift.
My mother called it a curse.

I loved my grandparents.
Like I said, they gave me this farm.

Grandpa taught me how to do everything.

I remember eating breakfast with them at 6:30 every morning
right here at this table.
I remember what they sounded like and I remember
what they smelled like and I am only here
because of how hard they worked all their lives.

People say I never married
but they are wrong. I married the farm.

I'm old now.
I got my social security card the day they killed Kennedy.
I remember that day. I will always remember that day.

For thirty-five years I had all I needed—my tractors, tools, and cows.

I always let the hired man off for Christmas.
I stayed here with the cows. I did the work.
Twenty-five years in a row I never saw my family at Christmas.
I ate Christmas dinner late at night
right here, alone at this table after I was done with the milking.

Earl came here as my hired man and stayed 16 years.
He could do anything. He could turn a lot of ground black in a day.
Towards the end
we used a step ladder to get him up on the tractor.

He would stay there all day—mowing or plowing or whatever.
He would pee right off the tractor.
When he died it felt like I had lost a brother.

I loved November, when the corn was picked,
the barn tightened up for the winter.
But toward the end, each year I got to wondering—
Do I have another year in me?

I am in the fall of my life.
I sold my cows in 2011. I enjoyed my cows while I had them.
It was a good experience. My cows were my family.

My brother and I don't get along.
He is a handsome man. Very Hollywood.
Had a couple wives but he is no happier than I am.

My dad had a little dog and he would bring him here
and the dog would spook my cows.
I asked my dad to leave that dog at home but he refused
so one day I told my dad not to come here anymore.
We finally made up but I didn't see my dad for years—for years...

One day in November we were filling silo and we ran late.
I always milked late but that night it was
after nine when I finished milking.
When I got done and the pipeline was washing
I thought to sit on a bale of hay
and take a little rest. I was just so tired.
I woke up in the middle of the night still on that bale of hay.
I knew right then the cows had to go.
I was just so tired.

I want happiness. I really do. I want to fit in.
I am an outcast. I want to fit into society.
You are better off with a gal on your arm.
I never had that but people think better of you if you are married.
They really do.

I have lived a selfish life. I just took care of myself and the farm.
I never raised a kid. I have lots of cash in the bank
but I should have—I never spent anything on anyone.

Give me a day with the sun shining and the wind blowing
and me up on the Farmall pulling the hay baler.
The bales tight and of good quality, flying up into the wagon.
Good tight bales of decent quality.
You can't beat that. You really can't.

I went in for my yearly checkup.
They looked in my ears and eyes
and down my throat.
They asked me questions.
Then they said I was depressed. I know I'm depressed.
Tell me something I don't know.

Say, do you have a card you can leave me?
I might want to call you sometime.
I know you are a busy man but you seem to understand.

You know, don't you?

No Human Sound

Back from the war
He rolled
Like a single column
Of smoke
East to west across a land
Gone strange
Took hold of a forgotten farm
Northern Richland County
A remote outpost
Holding
No human sound
But the low cry
That surged from his throat
Lost to the wind
And the woods
Where he walked
A circled path
That no man could track
And lay claim
To who and what
He no longer dared to be

Four

Ancestral

Somewhere tonight
The calves of the calves
Of the cows I milked

Are watching this same snow
Fall from a Wisconsin sky
Onto their beds of straw

Their wide eyes looking up
Unaware of the long heritage
That brought them to this place

Separated by miles and time
Yet held by a husbandry
Strong shared and unsevered

Estranged

We are
who we are
where we are
having stumbled
one step
at a time
through the fading
light
slipping again
and again
on the loosening
stones
hands feeling
for
but always
missing
the open
door
the way back
until
one day
the new day
turned into
every day
until all
that was close
became distant
as an island
looming
vast and strange
beyond
water no one
is able to cross

January 31, 2010

We slept
all the winter night.

Our bed
before the bare window

in the back room
of the hidden house.

Below, the valley
bright as day,

frozen snow, white
stars and moon,

so sure of our solitude,
until today,

hiking the woods trail
above the house,

we found in a cedar grove,
the fresh laid beds of two deer.

Dry Dirt

Just today
I felt myself fall out of love
with this land.

Turned my back
on cornfields rolled up
tight as pineapple.

All afternoon, listened
to the wind rattle the pasture gate.

I watched dust devils dance
across the bottom ground.

How many times can a man kick dirt,
swear it has never been so dry?

Now I drop decades
of tending crops and cattle
into a heap out back

pull the year shut
like one would
an old door on an empty barn.

Holy Water

Uncertain
Of what might come

Be it too much
Or too little rain

Summer hail
Or high winds

A haymow ignited
Or tractor overturned

We asked
In early spring

Father Gillespie
Walk the Shade Tree Lane

In his cachet and stole
Rosary in hand

Chanting
The Litany of Saints

Praying
Latin prayers to St. Isidore

Casting
Onto the freshly tilled soil

Holy Water
From a raised aspergillum

Changing Weather

This evening of gray fog—
the pines sullen
against the wind.

Black Angus cows—
calves at side,
leave the open fields,
pass beneath boughs
seeking shelter.

Beyond, fields of standing corn
await a late harvest—
leaves lingering
on a bare branch.

In this hour
moving toward dark,
all beings
moving toward home.

Shifting gears, I hurry
the old tractor through chores,
certain of snow
by morning.

Coming In

You stand at the window, watching
the year's first snow
sift down
through branches of pine.

Your hands white with flour,
kneading dough.

I hold wood
split for the fire.
Hold this moment most of all.

Close the door
against all time or trouble.

In simple silence, new snow
        and evening fall.

Bread rises.

We turn
        to each other.

Next Year

Knowing nothing else,
he signs the dotted line
securing another loan
with a second mortgage
on land he'll never own.
Calls co-op,
orders fertilizer, fuel, and seed.
Welds his broken-up equipment
back into one piece.
Stays out all night
in the black fields,
putting in a crop.
Worries and waits
for the rain
which comes too late.
Watches all June, July, and August
a weak stand
battle the dry weeds,
till harvest hauls in
half a crop
which pays one-third the bills.
He figures the loss
at $100 per acre.
Pushes a pencil
all the winter nights,
calculating how many more acres
he'll need
to make some real money
next year.

For Levi

When I no longer heard
Your footsteps in play
On the upstairs floorboards

I knew
You lay sleeping
Under wool

Tiny hands around a toy
Breath sweet through perfect lips

I stepped out
As far as the woodpile
Felt the first flakes falling

Looking up
I caught the winter sky
Reflected in the window of your room.

To My Deceased Parents

Each year, at year's end,
I turn inward
to think more of what was
than what is likely to be.

I stay in by the fire
near your picture, books,
things you left me.

I long for one more night
that I might ask the unasked questions
of who and why,
when and how.

It is the grown child's remorse—
haunted more by the unknown
than the known.

Chasing Chores

Sun on the south porch, the dog
dozing beneath.

Late September.

The dry weeds rustle
as the old mare limps from hot sun
to box elder shade.

The year's hay now in the barn.
The garden gone to seed and no one
home to notice.

Years back, three families
farmed 700 acres, milked dawn and dusk,
seven days a week.

My boys pulled on big boy boots,
chased chores sunup to
sundown.

Now some lives laid to rest, others
starting up in far-away cities.

While here, on land that still stays home,
I've stayed
to chase these chores alone.

Each year grinding down, spring
to fall, a bit harder
than the last.

Crisis Call

Just once
I'd like to be one of the haves
instead of the have-nots

Get a boost up
instead of a kick in the teeth

So tired of this cold rain
falling
by July it will all be dry weeds

I don't know my own kids anymore
Can't imagine lives beyond the hill

The wife long ago
forgot how to wife

When did she get this
bitter and mean

I have a twelve-gauge loaded

Think I'll take a walk
down through the woods

Take a walk
down through the woods

Cultivating

Day after day, year
in and year out,
I never left my father's farm.

Wore down dirt,
a straight path from house
to barn.

Opened each day
with pocket knife and pliers,
the ways my father taught me.

Out on the blacktop, men raced
breakneck speed
to jobs in town,

to worlds apart
from what could be measured,
from what could be held close.

While I steered
the old red tractor, carefully
cultivating my narrow rows.

Two hands on the wheel, eyes
tucked back
beneath my wide-brimmed hat

so not to rise up, look ahead
and veer off-course
into today.

old farmer

when the sun drops
behind the barn
giving his spot
by the garden
to shade
he limps out
to sit
where he can see
the whole farm
the fences
he strung
across pastures
where Holsteins
turned grass into milk
the fields
he plowed
and planted
and wrestled
out a crop
year after
year
until it all
became too much
and fell behind
into the life
he lived

Some Nights, My Father

would walk me
out
into the darkness
between the house
and barn

to show me
Cassiopeia
The Big Dipper
and the North Star

these things a child
must know

so that one day
should the world
veer suddenly
off course

he can walk
with his child
across the open
into the darkness

and point
to what is constant
illuminating
and true

The Fields in Winter

In this new life
brought on by death,
I cling to old routines
like the outstretched hand
of a friend.

Winter barely begun,
yet this cold
is the most intense I've known.
Deep in the night, the old house creeks like a dry branch.
I let the faucets drip, hearing
from my bed the pattering of pipes,
like another heartbeat
in the long darkness.

For no reason, I am up
at dawn, the instant coffee
cooling in the cup
while I pull on layers
of wool and flannel,
the heavy, five-buckle boots,
and stomp out across the snow
in the new light
to my barn of empty stanchions.
I feed my cats, and wonder
what now?

———————

A lifetime ago I plowed these fields
                         the first time
behind a matched team of Belgians
             named Sugar and Cream.

The leather reins in my hands,
my feet in the furrow, round
            after round,
together we paid down a mortgage
and raised up a crop—partners
            in the work of the land.

            Decades passed—still I smell
            horses cooling down at day's end,
            lather dripping from flanks.

I can't help but hold on
to old harness
slung over rafters
in an empty shed.

———————

November—
the last leaves
stolen from the trees.

I work alone
beneath a bare-branch sky.
Wandering from old house
            to old sheds,
an old man
at his woodpile,
building a mound
            against the coming cold.

I've gone back
to doing everything the hard way,
            the slow way,
just to prod time along.

The woodsmoke drifts
above the yard.
At night, fetching an armful
for the stove, I breathe deeply
the smoke
of the fire
that warms my home
built of wood cut, split, hauled
from my woods,
stacked beside my back door.

I hold to the simple pleasures
      of a simple life—
a chair pulled up to the fire,
memories burning in the wood.

―――――――

I feel foolish
but no one knows
I've set a straw bale
in the west doorway
of an empty mow—
  come to sit
  each evening,
watching the sun set over
  my land.

All these years, work
piled upon work,
I never took time
to just sit and watch a day
draw down.

Now I stay
till the lights of the distant town
glow like cat eyes
across the dark miles.

Tonight, heading for the house,
my solitary supper simmering,
I stopped
to hear the couplings of boxcars
echoing from a train yard
miles away.

I thought of our bodies—
    fifty-two years—
entwined all night
beneath a simple cotton quilt.

———

I look for you
each time, every time
I step in the kitchen door.

I hang my coveralls
outside,
leave my boots on the steps
as ordered.

Each night you stood
at the window
over the stove,
waiting for the barn lights
to go out,
for this tired man
to come in
smelling of cows and hay,
brought us a day
closer
to this day,
one of us gone and
one drifting alone.

———

Today, my young tenant farmer
rolled in
on wheels higher
than a man's head.

The roar
of his 250 horses
rattled the window panes
where I stood watching.

He plowed in a day
what I worked in a year—
then gone, his feet
never touched the soil.

I know him well, a good farmer,
he'll grow a good crop,
but I know, too,
he has heard their cold advice:

> "Get big, or get out.
> Farm fencerow to fencerow
> and when that's not enough
> tear the fencerows out."

And he believes them.

He is in love
with the new paint of agribusiness.
I stand aside, give him free rein.
In my day, I plowed
   a straight furrow too.
Filled my share
   of bins and barns
   with the labor of long days.

———

In the quiet hours, after lunch,
when the winds die down
and the sun slants sideways
through the bare trees,
I walk out
to my old red shed,
to stand at my battered workbench
stained by grease,
smelling of sawdust.

I crank the empty vise,
open and shut,
touch the cold steel wrenches,
chisels, pry bars,
hold the wooden hammer handles
worn smooth by hand.
These last years,
with everything breaking down,
wearing out,
I did more fixing than farming.
Thought we'd have to start working
at night
so the neighbors couldn't watch us
                          and laugh.
Now the cattle sold,
land rented out,
I sort the broken parts
of old machines,
scattered like bones
across the dirt floor
of my shed.

———

Months till spring,
I watch the snow,
   chop and carry wood,
practice my housekeeping.

Under the drifts,
outside the window
of the room where we slept
a half century
of nights
lie the little beds
of your garden.

Let others farm the big fields.
I'll tend to your flowers,
come walking
up the hill in summer,
a bouquet in hand.

Our Winter House

for Cheryl

Someday, when all these chores
are done,
I want to live with you, somewhere
far back, in a snow-covered lane.

In the shelter of evergreens.
In the silence of the migrated birds.
In a simple box of boards
we'll call our winter house.

Our time there marked only
by the falling flour bin
and the dwindling wood pile.

Rising each morning
to sweep the drifted snow
from the kitchen floor.

Pausing each evening
to watch the unbroken sunset
torch the west windows.

Then I will have no place
to rush off to
but to that place
where your eyes meet mine.

Nothing to hold in my hands
but the gold of each moment
lived alone with you, together,
in our winter house.

www.ingramcontent.com/pod-product-compliance
Lightning Source LLC
Chambersburg PA
CBHW031730290426
43661CB00140B/1476/J